THE
HEALING

HANNAH G. MILAN

Fulton Books
Meadville, PA

Published by Fulton Books 2022

ISBN 978-1-63860-232-3 (paperback)
ISBN 978-1-63860-233-0 (digital)

Printed in the United States of America

For those who have shattered and exhausted their hearts, pouring an abundance of love into anyone other than themselves, this is for you.

Contents

Preface

Love, in every form, is the most devastatingly beautiful thing to be acquired. Love never withers. Love never wanes or fades from the vibrancy that originates the very moment it is conceived.

The shattering reality of sharing that love, however, is the inevitable heartbreak to be suffered. The pain that can derive from fragmented love demands to be felt. I am well acquainted with the misfortune of having no other choice but to confront those fears. With the breaking, comes the ache that doesn't immediately rip you apart but, instead, over time, slowly wilts—like the petals from a Magnoliophyta.

Through these sorrows, I have reconstructed desolation into light. I have revived the flaccid, lifeless garden. I have unhinged the door and removed the barriers to expose my tangled mind. This is raw. This is real. This is vulnerability and passion.

Scripted in the pages of this book, you will discover various representations in reference to the many ways love can come into your life. I will reference the many masks love can wear and the avenues on which it can be hidden—like an ambush, quickly rushing into your life. For this very reason, you'll find that I've compared love to oceans, fire, flowers, art, and even inebriation.

While going through the motions throughout the years of heartache, I have sought refuge in many bottles of whisky, reading, and, oftentimes, creating chaos in my own life. I have made my fair share of mistakes. I have slipped; I have fallen; I've jumped without a safety net and a defective parachute. Though, through my experience, I have learned. I have developed. I have forced myself to never settle. I have pushed myself to find my worth. I have encouraged myself to accept nothing less than what I know I deserve. I rediscovered self-love.

I hope the words in these chapters give you strength and comfort to overcome your anxieties. The traumas do not ever entirely dissipate, but let this be a tribute that you are capable of taking control of your life again.

You will heal.

The Meeting

Red Candy Apple

My mouth watered—at the vision
of your lips.

My Favorite Art

Claude Monet
couldn't paint something
as beautifully intricate
as you.

Familiar

familiar

your scent,
your eyes,
your smile,
your charm,
your touch,
your skin,
your lips on mine,
your voice,
your love

familiar

Hinges of My Mind

When you oil the hinges of the mind,
don't shudder once you discover what you
said you were looking to find.
Don't be alarmed the deeper we dive.
You'll know my secrets, what I do—to keep myself alive.

Some of the doors will be harder to open,
some doors will stay closed,
those are ones I kept my "hope" in.

On the walls, you can find some dents and old memories,
listed, buried—
you may find my old enemies.

In the walls, in floor cracks,
you'll find what "slipped through,"
Loves lost, unfinished letters—to the people who mean the most.

As you go back down the hallway and approach the spiral staircase,
take a moment to appreciate the way my walls are shaped.
Not parallel or linear, not straight but ridged edged,
my mind has finally become a place I love,
instead of one I dread.

Make Me Feel

If every man were as capable as him,
no woman would ever be in need of anything—
ever again.

The things he made me feel…
everything.

Galactic Irises

I never understood getting "lost" in someone's eyes
until I was mesmerized, paralyzed by yours.

Happier Time(s)

If you gave me the time you give her,
you would be much happier with yours.

Surrender

This is me,
throwing my hands up.
This is me,
letting you in.
This is me,
giving my trust—my heart.

This is me.
I'm ready to break for you.

I surrender.

A Man

I saw a man.
I saw a good man.
I saw a drunk man.
I saw a handsome man,
a kind man.
I saw a man in distress.
I saw a strong man.
I saw a sexy man.
I saw a man full of passion,
he was driven.
I saw a vulnerable man.
I saw a tired man,
a hopeless man—
desperate for happiness.

I saw a man.
He was you.
I saw you—for you,
and I love you.

Can't Help Myself

What makes the forbidden fruit
so tempting and delicious?

The Loving

Unlike Before

Unlike the loves I've had before,
you didn't rush quickly. You took your time. You
didn't whisk me off my feet and pull me in like a tidal
wave. It wasn't about you and what you craved.
You were not violent. You were not rough—
like a whipping tornado spinning me in circles
until I was dizzy, blind, and confused.

Unlike the loves I've had before,
You were slow, calm, and steady.
Your embrace was soft and welcoming.
Your touch—gentle.
Your presence calmed me. You caressed me.
You made me warm.
The same warmth that you feel from a hot cup of tea when
you take the first sip—extending from the inside, out.
You offered peace. Comfort. Companionship.

Unlike the loves I've had before,
you enhanced my life, my spirit, my growth.
Unfamiliar—you brought to life parts of me I didn't even know.
Sleight of hand, you seized my heart—
unknowingly leading me into the greatest love I've shared in my life.

Unlike the loves I've had before,
the highlight of my life quickly became the black point
in which enclosed my empathy. I became numb.
Not emotionless rather simply present
from one moment to the next.
Never bothering to identify a glimmer of happiness—

knowing that desire is only received from your eyes and the way they smile at six a.m. on a Sunday when the sun peaks through the blinds—allowing the rays to rest upon your cheek.

Unlike the loves I've had before,
I've never lost you.
Unlike before,
I can never not be yours.

Fool(s) in Love

They say everyone has to be someone's fool.
I'm prepared to be yours.

Move with Me

she was the tide
and he was the moon.
always pulling her back,
causing her to tunnel underneath the surface
just so he could watch her beauty
as she arched up and roared, before she crashed,
gently floating back—onto the shore.

she was his puppet,
he loved her show.

Divine

Unlikely,
our paths would cross
yet align.

Nothing short of God,
it was divine
done by design.

Like a host to a flame
or when a farmer plants his seed,
once we allowed ourselves to love,
it started growing like a weed.

it made zero sense on paper,
the "unsolvable" equation,
no way to describe it
other than a "special occasion"

I don't know the "how" or the "why"
or even "when,"
but I'm glad our souls merged
exactly when they did.

I adore everything that you are.

It Always Will

it beats for you,
this heart.

Twin Flame

Me, the fire
you, the air.
Ironic
when you think of all the zodiac pairs.

I start as a spark,
you start as a breeze.
I develop a flame as your breath fuels me.

Your words, a match.
My mind, gasoline.
Your hands set me ablaze.
We made one hell of a scene.

As my flames start to roar,
you keep me at bay.
Yet not with intention
to smother or
suffocate.

You said from the beginning,
you would never dull my shine
though it makes little sense,
I know
you *are* my compatible sign.

Eclipse

Every time I see
the moon in the day,
I am reminded of our love.

An improbable occurrence
to exist simultaneously
in a world as transparent as ours.

It sends a striking jolt through your body
if you think about it.

The most unlikely of chances
a love like ours could ever emerge,
let alone flourish and prosper…

…but here we are.

Defeating the odds,
going against every voice of reason.
Illuminating the sky
Magnets, our lips
as we become
the
eclipse.

Eyes Never Lie

We lost sight of the moon
while counting the stars.

We got caught in the moment,
your eyes took me to Mars.

That's the thing about love,
it doesn't keep time
rarely does it have clarity,
reason or rhyme.

That's why they say you "fall"
into love,
rather "rise."

That's why they warn you
early on,
the significance of eyes.

Home

The fog we left on the windows
told the tale of our love.

Spontaneous,
free, and
untamed.

Unrushed,
you captivated me.

Fascinated by your charm,
I find myself lost in this enchanted paradise
that is only found in your eyes.

As I dive into your ecstasy,
the pressure rises with ease,
weight lifts off my shoulder,
and like a feather
I float into you.

Sinking until I brush your skin,
you seize me in one fell swoop.

Greeted with comfort and
overwhelming consideration,
an abundance of care.

I've known this paradise before,
but never was it my own.
Finally,
in your eyes,
I am home.

I Belonged There

I always liked the idea of belonging to someone.

but,

I loved belonging to you.

Paint Me a Picture

touched me with your eyes,
held me with words on your tongue.

you, the canvas
me, the paint
my lips, the brush
your breath, the water
your laugh, the muse

streaming aimlessly together
tangled, a mess
yet beautiful, our colors
complimenting the others'
infatuated with the effortless flow
flawless
sporadic but full…steady
unplanned, no direction
no stencil or pattern.
intertwined, yet parallel,
aligned

crawl toward me as I fade into you.
meshed, we blend—unite
entertainment, a pastime
we became art.

Muddy Water

We were always different.
We thrived in muddy waters.

What I Had Wished upon That Star

Dancing under stars,
wine on our tongues,
tangled in sheets
we made love.

Stay My Choice

I don't want to be left
with no choice,
but to spend my forever
without you.

Effortless Affection

I wish you could see
you are not difficult to love.

In fact,
loving you
is the easiest thing I've ever done.

Undying Love

I don't want to go through my life
without ever coming home,
and I want to come home to you.

Even when it's raining,
even when the earth quakes.

Even when the earth shatters
and the foundation starts to break.

I can handle the hurricanes.
I can surf the waves.

But I can't live this life without you,
I'll take this love to the grave.

Expire in Love

She asked,
"Would you love for fun?"
He replied,
"Wouldn't you?"

He later asked,
"Would you die for love?"
She responded through a smile,
"Wouldn't you?"

Secrets

Why are soft secrets
the hardest to lie in?

It causes me pain.
…you cause me pain.

Host of the Flame

I always liked playing with fire.
That was you and I'm burning alive.

Your flame found a home in me.
I thought I would survive.

Looking back on us,
as I turn to ash I wonder, *What did you learn?*
There's not a single thing I'd change
I think,
"What a lovely way to burn."

The Complex Minded

Why is intimacy more easily found at crowded
parties than small gatherings?

I believe because people are most entertained when believing
they have an audience to flaunt themselves around.

The mind becomes consumed with the thoughts of
desperately craving the opinions in others' minds about
themselves—so they boast. They wave. They entertain. All
in hopes they will catch the attention of the eyes that are
sought after by the majority—to claim their "victory."

And while the simple minded are infatuated with this game
they brand as pretentious affairs and love, the complex drift into
solitude. Alone with thoughts, passion, and an appetite for anything
on which they can feast their famished, philosophical minds.

Here is where they find each other. Here is where their minds
collide and slowly unfold their thoughts to the other—to reveal
the most intricate, cherished depth of their attentions.

Intimacy is much easier found in crowded spaces than small places.

There is more room for weak eyes to wander and very
few eyes that can hold the true elites' attention.

The Depth of the Ocean

The 36,200-feet Challenger Deep
is the oceans deepest point
and your love still was deeper than that.

The Feeling(s)

07/05/2014

Invisible strings connected,
seven years and they tighten
growing deep, becoming vessels for love
reeling us closer until we collide.

Never knowing what was in store.
Never existing in each other's world.

To go from nothing to everything
every turn we took was a path already formed,
unknowingly leading us to—not a place but a time.

The most simple interaction,
only wanting a temporary distraction
now fully engulfed in curiosity and excitement
Temptation
combust into intimate conversations.

Late nights, earlier mornings,
manifest into my daily dose
of ecstasy I label love…

…and to think I had ever been loved before you,
an illusion.

Chasing You

I always said I was tired and no one caught on.
I fed them the fable, old as time
of being exhausted from life
and displaying fake yawns.

Truth in point, it's really no lie.
I chase sleep.
I crave the feeling of my satin pillowcase
brushing the strands of my hair.
You see, every night
I run away in my dreams
and meet you there.

Again, I'll say
It's really no lie.

Chasing you left me nothing short of exhausted,
but it was always worth the price.

Save(d) Me

Gasping for air, no one could see
You rest your lips on mine and saved me from me.

Your eyes extend a portal, invite me to stay.

My weakness for you from that point only grew.

Hungry for mindless touch
your hands, I'd follow anywhere.

Awakened sensations, heightened stimulation
an addict born and cravings begin,
withdraws at night bleed into the day—
sleepless, exhausted—sweat streams like a river.
Turning cold,
Shivering.

Desperate, a fiend
you saved me from me.

Ultimate Incentive

Why do people *fall* in love?

Why can't we float?
Why can't we glide?

Why can't we sail?
Why can't we slide...
...or soar
or drift
or fly?

There is a daunting awareness
that people rarely mention.

While you slip,
it can feel freeing,
but you will also
feel tension.

The natural urge to brace the fall
will be the hardest of battles to fight.
The anticipation of "is this wrong"?
Or for once, should I risk
being right?

It's scary but rewarding,
once you choose to take the leap.
You may find
the one whose heart
may forever be yours to keep.

Held in Reserve for the Deserv(ing)

You are to me
a pin
to a grenade.

You keep me calm, composed,
contained,
ensuring I do not detonate
into self-destruction.

You,
being part of what I am composed.

You,
being the one thing keeping me from being exposed.

An Artificial Life with an Authentic Love

I keep myself fake busy with fake friends in a fake life,
keeping a job that I fake like,
always claiming I want love, knowing all love will be fake
if it is not yours,
especially when compared.

and no matter how hard I try to forget and move on
and take my life back into my own hands…

…I can never forget.

The taste of your lips
after two glasses of wine,
or the chills your fingertips gave me
sweeping down my spine.

I fake many things,
but
loving you isn't one.

Forever Home

Familiar in seconds, felt like an old friend
but we'd never had a beginning and we'd never had an end.

Learned most about the other when the world was asleep,
we stayed up for hours laughing until we couldn't breathe.

Peculiar—the way your hand fit in mine.
Like gloves or my rings, almost done by design.

You became my "safe place," my comfort, my home.
I hated parting ways and going home alone.

Reason and purpose, you gave to me—always excited
for the next time I'd see
your radiant smile as street lights grazed your face.
I wonder if you know, I still get that way.

Forever my lighthouse, for you led me home.
with you
is the greatest place
I've ever known.

Leading Light

Like a lighthouse to a sailor
when the siren sings her song,
I will extend myself to you,
so you can find your way back home.

I will not leave you to be stranded
or lost and all alone.
I will not leave you to be lured into
the depth of the unknown.

Tempting as it may be at times,
to drift off at sea and stay gone,
deep down, the only thing you want
is to be sought after
and found.

I will always lead you home,
You know you're safe with me,
and I'll remind you day after day if I need to,
I can love you *and* leave you free.

Thunder and Rain

You were like the thunder.
You were like the rain
coming fast from miles away.

You were like the ocean
a tidal wave
pulling me down to a darker place.

The night came quickly,
the moon pulled the tide.
I washed up onto the shore
surprised; somehow, I was still alive.

Seemed so harmless at first,
innocent, to say the least
that was before I dove your depth
and drowned in your sea.

You, My View

I could watch the sun set
a million times
and still be in awe at the view.

I feel the same
when I look at you.

More

I couldn't help but think of all of places I hadn't touched.
Places my lips hadn't kissed,
my hands hadn't grazed,
the places my tongue didn't taste,
the place in your heart I'd always chase.

I wanted you to want me
and you did,
but I wanted more.

I always wanted you more.

Never End

You were the art gallery
the book I could read over and over again,
never getting bored.

Always excited to turn the page…

We were the book.
We are the story.

We can never end if we are in words…

…and maybe that's why I'm writing this.

Held

To my mind,
a hostage.

To my thoughts,
a hostage.

To my pride,
a hostage.

To my life,
a hostage.

Fight for You

right when you feel there's nothing more,
go to war.

Ticking Clock

You seem to have a magic power
when I'm with you, time stops.
When you're close, it slows
and when you're gone,
my heart drops.

Beautiful, yet dangerous
frozen in time, caught.
Enhancing every memory made,
have you ever *felt* a thought?

What I would give
to freeze that moment,
the very first time
our eyes locked.

Knowing what I know now,
it'd be a chance to choose my fate.
Would I dive head first into you
or would I cling to my clean slate?

Sometimes I wonder what I'd choose to do,
if given the chance again,
would I unlock the door and let you in
or would I leave it at a wave and grin?

I Thought I Was Being Cautious

If I cared,
I would never stay long enough to show it.

A "do not touch" display,
close enough to see,
but just enough out of reach.

I'd say, "I want held,"
but couldn't stay still long enough
to be caressed,
embraced.
Anything that would make me feel wanted,
an estranged feeling—
foreign, unknown...

Petrified, I allowed myself to fall,
unaware of the feelings to be felt
luring me into an abyss
of everything I never knew I always wanted.
My wildest dream.

Pulled me down,
into wonderland—
magical, surreal...

...only to wake up to find that
none of it was real.

This is why my hope—and even dreams of mine—die.

The Leaving

Sin

I should've never called.
I let you back in,
but what was I to do?

You always were my favorite sin.

(Wo)man Down

Half drunk on a Sunday with faith running low,
not even dressed but places to go.
No motivation, severe lack of sleep,
growing more tired as I'm turning weak.
I miss my own smile, my laugh, my joy.
It hurts me to realize you used them like toys.
Exuding confidence, no need for a boost,
Still you took mine and left my pride bruised.
Played the role of a fool, more than once—even twice,
I have no idea why I lost sleep all those nights.
I thought you were different; your soul spoke to mine.
I understand now, why they say love is blind.
Thought we'd make it to "I do" instead of "over"
Comparative to being drunk and then suddenly sober.

With reckless abandon, you loved me wild.
I was truly convinced one of you would file...

You brought me so far, got me so high.
I will never believe our love was a lie.

But you damaged my spirit, gashed me open to bleed.
Scared and alone, you said you'd be there for me.
Yet, on those late nights, you were no longer found.
I accepted our ending, my white flag on the ground.

The Smoke Will Remain in Your Eye

Ashes, you say,
we all fall down.
Yet before we turn to ash,
you put the fire out.
That's the issue with you,
you can't handle the heat.
Every time you get close, you panic,
you flee.
You run away from the passion,
scared to get burned.
I had a feeling I would be
the hardest lesson you've learned.

You Were Not Made for Me

Bits and pieces, then all at once
you came into my life and
breathed breath into my lungs.

You made me think you were a treasure, but
this could not be true.
I had a life before you.
I know I don't need you.

But over time, we shared our feelings;
we talked about all we could have.
I started believing what we had was true;
it made it difficult to turn my back.
Alike in every way,
but they say "opposites attract."

The love I had for you was real;
it always will remain,
but I had to get away from you;
you were driving me insane.

And now that we have severed,
even though my heart does break.
I made the right decision for us.
I made no mistake.

I'll always want the best for you,
forever that will be true,
but illusions aren't meant to be lived in forever;
it could never be me and you.

"Love" Me to Death

Thought I was falling in love,
until I fell at your feet.

I knew when I met you that you'd destroy me.
I even told you that once,
I begged you to let me go.
I couldn't pull myself away.

Asphyxiated by what I perceived as your love.

Your charisma, my noose,
while I begged you
to just let me go.

Heartbre(ache)

Do you know heartbreak?
Do you know her sting?
Does anyone *truly* know what I mean?
Do you feel her ache?
Do you hear her scream?
The kind that leaves you wondering if it's just a bad dream.

I've grown all too familiar.
I live in that place.
My fear bleeds into my days.
There's no way to escape.

Do you know heartbreak?
Do you know her sting?
Can you feel my ache?
Can you hear my scream?

You're Hurting Me

What feels the best to you
hurts the most for me.

Drown in My Sea

Rain drops.
Puddles.
Oceans.
Consistency matched but differing depth.
Joy and sorrow belong to each one.
We need water to grow, but we also need sun.

Too much of good things are still known to kill.

I am the storm,
the wind,
the rain.
The blaze from the lightening,
the bellowing thunder.

You pursued a hurricane.

Cold and dark yet you ran toward me.

You pursued this disaster.
You encouraged this destruction.

I Can't Let Go

Even with my hands tied,
I'm still reaching for you.

The Parting

The bittersweet,
in our last hour.

We laughed
and we cried,
slow danced,
laid side by side.

We listened to music,
we made love,
but the feeling of knowing what was coming,
we couldn't get rid of...

...and though we knew our time would be short,
that day we said it all.
I'll never be able to not see your face,
the last time going down that hall.

Our love is everlasting.
It's true—it never ends.
Once the best of lovers,
now parting ways saying "we can be friends."

I wanted nothing more than you,
in my entire life.
I reminisce on the days.
I thought I'd be your wife.

But all good things must come to a close.
They say what goes up must come down.
I loved you then and I'll love you forever,
and I'll keep praying you'll come back around.

Reunify

Eyes swollen from crying,
exhaustion sets in.
Can't keep myself from wondering
how you have been…

I want to reach out,
but know it's best I don't.
I crave so badly just to hold you,
it hurts to know I won't.

Through music and dreams,
I can never seem to outrun you.
Makes me never want to wake up,
and some days,
I'm shocked I still do.

Without you,
my heart aches.
I'm drowning in pain.
I feel like I can't breathe.
I feel like I'm going insane.

They say if you love something,
you need to let it go,
but the hardest thing for me
is not being able to say, "Hello."

I hope
as we take on this journey,
you always feel me by your side.
I hope for us to come back together,
unite, instead of divide.

Welcome

I knew the end was near,
and I was okay with that.
It was the anticipation
of not knowing when.

Is this the last time,
or will you come again?

Poor Sport

A sport to you,
breaking hearts.

…just because you could.

I Can't Breathe

One of the most difficult things I've attempted
is forgetting you.

I don't want to,
but I'm suffocating in our memories.

The Fallout

I remember the day I fell out of love.
Snowing and freezing, my mind was made up.

Confused how it happened, I wanted to stay,
…maybe too much time to think while you were away?

I still love you now, and I'll love you forever,
but time working against us caused our future to sever.

I'm the one that fell out and that eats me alive
because I didn't mean to, but part of me died.

While the way you loved me brought me joy and laughter,
when things got rocky, you left my emotions a disaster.

Distraught at first, thought our love would transcend,
but I've finally accepted; it's best that we end.

State of Mind

They always talk about how to fix a broken heart, but
let's talk about when someone breaks your mind.

What do you do?
I'm desperate to know.
What eases that pain?
How do you mend a shattered mind?

You can fix a broken heart.
Time can heal a heart,
but time for a mind
can be fatal.

You

You were
all I ever wanted within arm's reach.
Everything I had dreamed to feel, taste.
The very soul I had fantasized my whole life of encountering.

You were
Warm. Gentle. Soft.
Inviting. Pure. Raw.

Your love, exquisite.
Natural.
Seamless.

You were all I ever wanted.

You were
the one that showed me true love;
the one that broke my heart.

You were
my one and only.

I was yours,
but you were hers,
regardless of how desperately
you wanted to be mine.

Asphyxia

Losing you felt much more like losing myself.

You had become my sunshine.
My good days.
My happy place.
My laughter.
My contentment.

Losing you felt like losing the very air in which I breathe.

And now, I am left to suffocate.

The Mourning

After You

After you,

I know how it must feel to a girl that goes colorblind only after
knowing how beautiful the world is in pastels and neon.
To see everything vibrant, full of life and love, exuding through
every pore of sky onto the ground on which it rests—to
magnify every good thing in this—all too grim—world.

After you,

I lost color. Blue eyes are simply a darker grey than the rays I
catch from oceans glistening in the reflection of the sunlight.
Greyscale shades—white to black—almost as if I struggle to see the
purpose of such beautiful silhouettes—of what beauty I once knew.

After you,

Nothing is the same. Rather bland than vibrant.
Shades of cool with no tones of warmth.
The embers that rise from the fire that once mesmerized me with
their glow, now blend with the ashy sky to which they float.

And so I go on.

In hope that someday, those colors can be restored.
The thorns on the roses protruding even enough vibrancy
to never depreciate their value and beauty.
Blue eyes become the ocean, rather than a comparison to get lost in.

Meanwhile, I freeze—and pray the warmth
consumes me—before I am ice.

DOA

Homeless, offtrack,
with no destination in mind
just trying to take it
one day at a time.

That's where you found me.
Alone and unarmed,
I had no intention to cause any harm.

Exhausted from the night before,
I had told no one of the cross I bore.

I wasn't seeking attention,
just shelter and warmth,
one full plate and a coat
to get me through the storms.

I had fled from my parents
just to run toward my demise.
I sought shelter in a home
where I was scorned and despised…

…and maybe I was wrong to think I would ever feel safe again,
but
when you get to the point I was,
there was nothing I wouldn't bargain
for a home with "welcome" signs
and a "come on in" doormat.

I still found that solace
though it looks different
in granite,
my gravestone now my doormat.

They Always Do

The question is never *if* they will stay,
it's just a matter of how long they will stay
before leaving.

Peace Deprived

Missing you
was the cause
of my
insomnia.

My anxiety derived
from my wandering mind.
What if you were really the one?

Liberating

And as I shed these tears,
they act as fluid on a windshield
once brushed to the side,
my vision clearer than before.

I never needed him.
I simply wanted him.
I desired his time and attention.
I craved his love.

I enjoyed what we shared,
lavished in temporary euphoria
but there was liberation
in letting you go.

I'm Still Up at 2:00 a.m.

Coffee and laughs at 2:00 a.m.,
it's hard to believe we started as friends.
We fell in love, didn't take long,
now you've left me all alone

I just can't sleep
without you next to me.
I stay up all night counting stars
'til I can't see.
Always haunting me is your love that lingers here.
Living life without you was always my biggest fear.

Not even miles between us could make a difference now.
Left with so many questions but the hardest one is *how*?

How could you fall so deep
in love with me to leave?
I guess I didn't mean as much to you,
as you to me.

Now, I see.

Fade

Our time,
then
our love,
then,
our memories…

We'll fade.

One Is Never Enough

Lips like the rim of a whisky glass
inviting, yet the glass is so shallow.

Even at the bottom of the barrel,
I am always left wanting more.

How Many Fish Are in the Sea?

I find myself
never quite ready,
never quite able
to love someone else.

You were my one.
You may have been my only.

That petrifies me.

One Day Soon

One day soon, you'll look for me.
You'll search high and low,
in the faces of everyone, especially people you know.

You will chase certain feelings because they'll remind you of me,
but if you ever get close, they'll be quick to flee.

You'll crave certain songs and dissect the lyrics.
You'll go to all of our old spots
hoping to still feel "it."

You will smell my skin and try to breathe me in,
I wonder how you feel to know you'll never hold me again.

When reality sets in,
you'll realize what you missed.
The one difference is
you'll have misery,
I'll have bliss.

Forever you'll be chained to the life you've always known.
Same town, same job
all of which I've outgrown.

One day soon, you'll be in agony,
you will discover, you will never find me.

The sooner it's accepted, the sooner you're free,
but never question this: *with you* is still where I'd rather be.

Caged

Forever wed to a body in which my spirit does not fit.

In every aspect of my life,
I feel like a bird.

Born to fly
but with clipped wings.
I am solely limited to a fraction of my own potential.

Essentially,
this is my greatest form of torture.

I watch the world around me increase with pace and tempo
while I am stuck,
window watching my dreams pass me by.

The Constant Battle

You will always be a battle I fight.
Did I do enough? Should I have fought harder? Waited longer?

You will forever be the one—and my mind dwells—
Shredding through the pages of our memories
as fast and as often as I can, so I don't forget a thing,
not one detail of who we were
when we were together.

The greatest version of myself existed, when I existed with you.

The truth is, I always left a candle burning for you.
I still don't know if it was in hope that you would
see some light from my bedroom window and
have the courage to knock on my door
or if it was in memory of you…and everything we surrendered.

You left me with so many unanswered questions.

Who has your heart?
Is it well?
Does she love you—the real you—the way I do?
Does she even know you—or care to—the way I did?
How's your mom? …and your sister?
Do you miss me?
Are you empty?
Is it just me?

Shards of Heart

Why
is it easier to fall apart,
be destructive,
crumble to pieces?

You make it impossible to hold you.
No one could ever hold you…
…not all of you.

You break
leaving debris,
pieces of yourself everywhere you go.

From one heart to the next,
you spread yourself thin.

It's impossible for anyone to know your entirety.

Miss Me Yet?

Do you miss me yet?
Have I crossed your mind?

I'm laying here tonight,
thinking about your eyes
always so kind,
always inviting…
makes me wonder about this love
and why we're hiding.

I don't have much time,
and I'm tired of fighting.

What was once so strong now feels like it's dying.

Put your hand in mine
while I
cry and close my eyes.

Keep me in this lie,
kiss me one last time.

"Never much time,"
but always denying that this love we made
leaves one of us dying.

I can't turn back time,
and I'm tired of trying.
We weren't made to save this love.
Can we stop lying?

Singe(d), Not Yet Scorched

Torched,
now blistered
from the flame that drew me in.

What am I to do
when
the same flame that scalds me is my comfort,
my only warmth
the only thing caressing my skin?

…wrapping around me tightly
and keeping me driven?

I know I'll freeze
without the flame,
the blaze keeps me alive,
but I can't
hold onto embers
and
somehow expect to thrive.

Self-Harm

A brief exchange
several years ago
led to intertwined souls,

but before we could ever transpire,
I had to hit an "all-time-low."

From the moment we met,
you were calm, so collect,
your firmness was noted,
but your smile was direct.

Years later,
when you placed your hand in mine,
that very moment, I knew—

if you'd commit that hand to me (forever),
there's nothing we wouldn't get through.

So hesitant to take that chance with me,
even knowing we'd have a grand life.
I felt cut open and wounded
until I realized,

it wasn't me you left
to bleed
and cry.
You really only played yourself—
you cut yourself with your own knife.

Tug of War (Mind and Heart)

I never could escape you.
Up for days, I couldn't sleep
with the prominent fear that you would find me.

Even still,
you'd find ways—if not in my dreams,
to show up in songs
and every movie scene.

Chaotic as it is,
You'd think I'd walk away.
You'd think I'd have learned a lesson,
You'd never think I would have stayed.

Yet, every time I slip into these dreams,
I run to you.
As if there is some horizontal gravity
drawing me in and forcing me closer
until I am
shoved into your embrace.

Always alluring,
exactly as I remember.

It takes everything in me to fight
the impulse, desire
to sink back into our pattern,
our routine of
unrequited
love.

Back to Me

You told me in some of your last words that
you would find your way back to me.
You promised in a way that begged me to believe you.
I believe you wanted to.
I believe you tried,

but I think along the way you got lost.

Your mind started telling you the fight was too hard,
the road was too long,
the sacrifice was too significant.

You never fully gave up,
you always showed up
bringing just as much, if not more
than the day before…

and maybe, some day
that will be our saving grace.

Maybe, you'll find your way.

Me in Her

You will spend
the rest of your life
trying to find me
in her.

It's unfortunate.

'Til Death Do Us Part

This love.
Our love.
Your coffin,
or
mine?

Satisfactory

Blank canvas to painter,
a pen to a poet
imaginations free-flowing,
there's no way to slow it

therapeutic, an outlet
for when no one's around,
to help you process your feelings
on days you feel down.

An escape for many,
a home for more
either way,
it opens a door.

Behind that door,
pillow and bed
a tranquil place to lay your stress,

as the words left unsaid
glide onto paper,
weight lifts of your chest
as they now rest
in the book of the life we once shared
now only to be read.

I've Tried, but I Can't

You left,
and
I haven't stopped thinking about you.
I haven't stopped missing you,
and I damn sure have never stopped loving you.

I'm Scared to Do It Again

You used to make me feel so good, so valued.
You made me feel so loved that now every time I get remotely close
to that feeling, I get scared.

I get scared to even feel at all…

because you made me feel like the only woman in the world,
but look at where that landed us.

You Haunt Me

Haunting
the "what could have been"
with you.

Snowflakes

I don't know
what to think
of the snow
mid-float,
glistening
as is dissipates
into air.

Where does it go?
What does it leave?
Is it only temporary?

The more I ponder,
I relate.
It makes sense in a way.

The most beautiful things are never meant to stay.

Mirage

Drowning
unphased at first,
the panic sets in after the third wave knocks me down.

Tunneling deeper from the surface,
confusion sets in.
No sense of direction
as I float, no
sink,
into the depth of the unknown.

Finally, accepting the surface is much
further than I had remembered.

No longer catching small rays of sunlight
through my clenched eyelids.

Lung full of water—weighing me down,
unable to breathe—
the clutch around my ankles tighten as gravity pulls harder…

and as I settle onto the bed of the plushy ocean floor,
I become just another casualty
to your tsunami of emotions—needs,
that you presented as love—I couldn't identify
a mirage.

Illicit Love

I wagered for a heart
knowing it was on borrowed time.

I knew your heart was never mine.
It would never be mine to love.
It was never mine to intertwine with
or connect to
or explore.

That's what keeps me up at night.

That's where my mind starts to slip
into an endless, revolving door
of all the questions left unanswered.

Was any of it even real?
Do you feel how I feel?

Did you want to be mine?
Was it a waste of my time?

Are you as lost without me
as I am without you?

Do you regret me?

Is there anything I can do?

Can We Go Back?

Let's start over
be strangers again.
Revisit the places
we've already been.

You tell me your name
and I'll tell you mine.
I'll tell you my favorite drinks are
bourbon and wine.

Let's relearn each other
the things we already know.
Your favorite season, your birthday
and how you love when it snows.

Let's go back to the night you first said, "I love you."
Fall in love all over, make memories, talk
about the things we want to do.

Find a little café and go there for brunch.
Make it "our special place" and go once a month.

Let's come up with new jokes, laugh harder and dance.
This time, let's be patient
and give each other a second chance.

In a World We Couldn't Be

Reclined in our affair,
we tangled.

We grew too comfortable as we grew closer into each other's skin.

The two of us longing for—no, relying on—our love
to carry us through every trial,
every twist of events that we knew would soon unravel
and expose our endeavor(s).

That evident love.
That strong, unbreakable, indestructible love
all of which remained,
while we were forcibly pried apart by our respective lives
that required us to play
much different roles than we had desired for ourselves.

That's the funny thing about love…
once it's had, even miles apart,
it lingers.

Why Couldn't You Choose Me?

I would've done anything for you,
and in fact, I did.

I displayed my love for you loudly, daily.
I was present—body and mind.
My efforts never ceased.

My ambition and drive to achieve a future with you,
never crippled.

You never were able to give me the same.
The life, the love you said I deserved.
You claimed you wanted to be the one,
that you had never loved someone's soul the
way you effortlessly loved mine.

Eager and willing to show me the world yet
bound to a life you chose over ours.

It was never enough for you to change.
Our future's fate in your hands
only for you to surrender our "could've been."

You must've grown tired.

That seems to be the only explanation I can concoct
to only slightly remedy my mind from the constant
ache for your breath to graze my neck once more.
For your fingertips to trace my cheek.
For your lips to gently collide—and melt—into mine.

For your eyes to raise from your rested gaze only to connect with mine in a way in which no words needed to be spoken.

You must've grown tired…
but you should know, I'm still sleepless.

The Healing

Heal

In leaving, there was a certain relief.

In the way my heart broke, there was a sense of comfort.

I have been here before.
The broken can be restored,
but a heavy heart from waiting could never heal.

Mirrors on the Wall

I wonder the stories my mirror could tell.
Would it tell you I'm heaven or would it tell you I'm hell?

Would it tell you of glimpses on days when it rained?
The sadness, depression—the misery and pain...

Are more of the pictures darling and quaint?
The days filled with teacups and canvases and paint...

Did it store in its memory all the years of my youth,
Christmas mornings in PJ's and when I lost my first tooth?

If you looked at my mirror, what would you hope to see?
The days that I'm sad, or the days I love me?

To me—it seems—you'd rather me cry,
than to know that without you, I'm still doing alright.

If I could glance back on all of my days,
I'd choose to go back on the days that seemed gray.

Not to sit there in silence and unpack and stay,
but to see myself pray and still not be okay.

For it was in those moments, I regained my power.
I picked myself up, wouldn't let myself cower.

You may think you know me, but mirrors know all.
I'll get up ten times if nine times I fall.

The Void

You took pieces of me
and when I put myself back together,
you will have those pieces.
There will be voids, yet
that will be the whole.

Who I am now as a whole,
the new whole
with the void from the pieces
you took from me.

One Hundred of Me

Intact, complete
unbroken
pristine, one piece.

I dreamt of being that girl.
The one that looked put together.
Cute outfits and purses and flawless falling curls.

The reality is, I'm nothing close to "her."
I'm messy, unorganized,
but it's what I prefer.

I'm real, authentic,
genuine and kind.
Rich in the ways that matter,
I won't flip on a dime.

I'm solid as a boulder,
some say thick as one too,
but let me give you a tip or two…

"Chubby" or "Skinny," they'll always chime in,
be proud of every flaw and all your achievements.

Do not conform to society,
don't let them tell you what to do.

Do what makes you happy and
don't ever discount *you*.

Full Picture

Take the negative,
let it sit in the dark;
give it a few days,
a few weeks…

Then flip the switch,
turn the light on

…and stand back in awe at the fact:

sometimes darkness is exactly what is needed to fully develop.

Whispers to the Moon

Oh, moon,
how you know me.

We share so many secrets.

When We Broke

When your heart broke,
time stopped.

Knowing I was the reason for your pain.
Your distress.
Your discomfort.
Your agony.
Your loneliness.

Sometimes, I feel as if I'm stuck in that moment
feeling every preexisting crack of your heart finally give way
and shatter into an infinity of pieces.

When you broke, it broke me,
but staying would've killed me.

Which Is True?

I believed you were crazy.
You believed you exhibited love.

Excuse me,
if it's all a bit hazy,
in my mind.

Sprout

There is no growth in comfort.

Establish your roots,
then

Sprout.

You Destroyed Who I Was Then but Thank You

You hit me like an earthquake.
Coming in quickly, shaking me violently,
until I shattered into pieces,
crumbling at my very foundation
losing pieces of myself in every new crack
pieces I will never get back.
Therefore; pieces I can never restore.
After you, I will never be the same,
and I'm grateful for that.

I Didn't Mean to Love Him More

Sometimes it takes two hearts
to realize you only need one.

Never Give Up

To fail
means you had to try
and that alone is such a large accomplishment.

Interior Design(er)

Cracks in the walls,
creaking wooden floors
run-down walls
and holes in the doors.

No running water
left abandoned for some time.
No light could peak through
the slanted window blinds.

Yet still
you came in,
despite the rust on the lock,
hung up new curtains,
dusted and mopped

rolled some fresh paint
and put portraits on the walls,
moved in blankets and beds
and after several more hauls

you conformed the shells
of this house
to a home.

You gave it life and purpose.
Now, finally
your own.

Drift

I've always struggled with letting go
of memories,
emotions,
and people.

But there is beauty in letting your pink balloon fall from your
wrist and holding it between two fingers—right before allowing
it to rise and float—drifting to a place unknown—ascending
to the sky until it's not only out of reach but out of sight.

There's power in that.
There is freedom in that.

Untie yourself.
Release the past.

Rise.
Float.
With no guidance or direction.

Free yourself from the wrist that has you wrapped so tightly.

Soar through your life.
Reach the height of your potential.

There is only one string holding you down.

Let it go.

You Owe It to Yourself

So I left.
I packed my things and moved out.
I hesitated at first.
I hated myself for that.

Part of me wanted you to stop me,
show me why I should stay.
I cried.
I wallowed,
probably too long,
in self-pity…
but then came a day that I had enough.

Hoisting myself up from the kitchen floor,
I wiped my own tears
and broke free from the chains
that kept me emotionally bound to you.

I stood tall.
For the first time in my years with you,
I was free from your mental restraint.

With ease, I inhaled deeper than ever before.
At last,
I could breathe unrestricted.

It takes a lot to start over,
to realize what you deserve and
actively work toward allowing yourself
to flourish and grow.

But you're allowed to give yourself a chance at the life you deserve.
You are not selfish for wanting the very best for yourself.

At Your Convenience

You didn't love me.

You loved how "into" you I was.

You loved my loyalty,
my willingness to go to extremes for your happiness.
You loved what I did for you;
how I made you feel.

You loved a lot of things about me, but
you never loved me…

and you always knew.

Do Better

Sometimes I think we get distracted,
and we fight for the wrong things.

Fight to be decent.
Fight to be respectable,
to be brave.
Be exquisite.
Fight to be the person that sets the standard and set the bar high.
Fight to do right even when the wrong is easier.
Fight to be better than the version of yourself you were yesterday.

Stop fighting with each other.
This isn't a competition.
Everyone you encounter is doing the best they can.
Lift them up. Does it really matter if you like them or not?

Take care of people.

You never know
who could be put in a situation to take care
of you someday.

Where Tomorrow Is Today

"One day" became today.
Twelve years overnight,
I awakened to find all of my "tomorrows"
directly in front of me.

All of the "I'll feel better tomorrow"
and "Tomorrow will be better"
finally happened,
simultaneously,
suddenly,
and amazingly with perfect timing.

I made it to "tomorrow."
The sun is shining,
I am glowing.
I am well.

I'll rest peacefully
as I know,
I survived.

I made it.

You Are the Romance

Romanticize your life.

Everything about your day,
maximize it.

Your coffee in the morning and
your cup of tea at night,
The first day of spring
when you crack all of your windows,
the days you spend alone, driving aimlessly in your car.

Bring it all to the forefront.

Be present with your anxieties.
Acknowledge them.
Feel them.
Confront them.

And then
annihilate them.

I'm Proud of You

Note to my fifteen-year-old self:
we made it.

Hunger

My heart had never been more starved for love,
affection,
attention.

I kept my walls up,
I worked tirelessly to build them.
Higher, stronger, and with much more density than ever before.

No one would get through.
I simply wouldn't allow it,
not after the last time.

This heart could not bear to be broken again...

...but you appeared out of nowhere with everything I wanted,
extending love from your eyes
and regard with your hands.

I told you we could be friends.
It made me feel safer,
used that title
like a force field to blanket my heart.

I knew not to trust the words,
solely the actions behind them
and that's where you fooled me.
You showed up every day,
you sent flowers,
you remembered the anniversaries and my birthday,
and you took me out—not just on the town but
from my own shell I had hibernated into...

You put forth so much effort,
every day,
every single day,
just to force me to feel the brokenness all over again.

I thought I'd hate you forever for that,
but I don't.

Today, I chose to forgive you,
and every day since,
I have chosen
forgiveness.

Overdose

Presented to me as medication,
a cure,
Only to realize, as I get worse,
it's poison.

I took you.
Little questions were asked.
Blindly confiding in what was scripted to me,
took you at face value,
trusted I could give you a chance,
"What's the worst that could happen?"

And maybe that falls on me;
maybe I should've done my research.
Due diligence was not prioritized,
let alone
on my mind.

I wanted to feel better;
desperate for relief,
I took handful after handful,
believing
I could convince myself
it wasn't as bad as it seemed,
it wasn't controlling me,
I wasn't changing,
I wasn't irritable, moody, and callous.

It's always been like me
to have to learn the hard way;
come hell or high water,
I had to see for myself.

I've always heard to be cautious,
Addiction then overdose;
It's never your intention,
You never think it will be you…

…I get it now, though. I really do.
I understood when I overdosed on you.

If You Won't Do It, I Will

I think this is the part
where I let my mind take over, fight my heart,
shed some tears,
let you go,
and finally…

…finally put the energy I've been giving you back into myself.

I deserve it.

What Really Sets You Free?

They say the truth sets you free,
so
why, if our love is true,
are we stagnant and caged?

And They Thought We Were the Fools

We had the whole world
believing we were entirely and utterly oblivious
to the other's existence…

…when we were the two that knew each other better than anyone.

You've Made Your Point, I Just Hope It Was Worth the Cost

I feel like I am strapped to a chair
every time I attempt to stand up
to you.

I want to run after you.
I want to hold your hand.
I want to experience this life with you,
but
as I start to gain clarity,
I'm beginning to remember...

...you're the one that bound me here
to sit,
to stay.
To watch and
suffer.

...and love doesn't do that.

Love isn't forceful solely to prove a point.

You Think You're "Disappointed"?

If you are disappointed in who I am,
let me clue you in.

When I love, I love with my all. I love at 100 percent. I don't
know how to love less than entirely, and oh! I have loved.

When I am lost, I am low. I lose every sense of direction. I
lose my mind. I lose my heart, and oh! I have been lost.

When I break, I hit rock bottom. I tear myself down when
I think there isn't a "lower" low. I cry, I scream, and I beg in
prayer to God. I feel my pain, and, oh! I have broken.

So when you think you have the privilege of merely
having an opinion of me, just remember this:

You didn't see me when I broke. You didn't find me when I was
lost. You didn't see the way I loved. You didn't see me live…

…and oh, have I lived.

You cannot fathom my experiences or who I am
now based on the things I've made it through.

You don't get the privilege of feeling anything
for me, for I am but a stranger to you.

Put Her to Rest

I closed the casket.
I sealed the lid on the urn.

I buried and sprinkled every last part of who she
used to be so she could be found nowhere.

That girl died. It was better this way.

The girl with naive dreams and eyes that twinkled at the
sound of fairytales when the princess found her prince.

The girl that thought life would happen *to* her
instead of making life happen for herself.

The girl that was guiltless and allowed herself to be
subjected to a stampede of society's ideas of perfection.

She died.

Though, when she expired, it gave space for the matured, lively,
happier, stronger version of herself to resurrect into life.

The girl that laughs more. The girl that smiles. The girl that
knows her worth. The girl that doesn't back down and cower.
The girl that makes her own dreams come to life. The girl
that knows what love is and isn't. The girl that knows not to
accept anything less than worthy and doesn't feel selfish for
putting herself first. The girl that becomes her own fairy tale.

That girl lives freely now.

That girl is doing things. That girl is enjoying life and is full of spirit, spunk, and fight, and she is well

…

…and she is me.

Swim

The many tears I've cried
created the oceans he swam
to find my soul.

Those tears were the gateway to being loved generously
and being left wild.

You broke me just enough to let him in.

Homeless

They say that home is where the heart is,
but my heart is in so many places.

It is torn, it is scattered, and it is everywhere.
When I go to find her and ask for directions,
I only find myself driving in circles.

Peace

To make a long story short,

I made it to the exact place I am meant to be.

Untruth(s)

The lack of truth in everything correlated with us was too much.

Superwoman Power

"If you could have any superpower, what would you choose?"

I used to get asked this question all the time.

I've noticed, as I've grown older, my
answers have changed with time.

But now?

I wish I could stall time and
pause certain moments—
That I could become gravity and
Hold these moment down as I exist in them,
never having to worry about when they will slip away.

By Heart

I know how you take your coffee
and all your favorite songs,
the significance of the Carolinas
and that you hate admitting you're wrong.

I know the way your chest feels to my cheek
when I lay my head to rest.
I know the way you look at me
When promising to give me your best.

I know your go-to bourbon,
and I know where you fall apart.

I know the most exclusive version of you.

I know you by heart.

Or Was That a Lie Too?

I know nothing more true than being
foolishly in love with you.

Everything in Me

When I first saw you,
it took everything in me not to touch you.

When I heard your laugh,
it took everything in me not to stare too long at the purity.

When I saw your smile,
it took everything in me not to kiss you.

When I kissed you,
it took everything in me not to fall madly in love with you.

When I fell madly in love with you,
it took everything in me to show you my depth,
my complexity…

…and when I saw your complexity,
your love,
your smile,
your soul,

it took everything in me.

Resting in Conflict

So I threw a funeral.

I spoke of our memories,
brought some old pictures,
and remembered our love…

…and then
I let it go.

Overwhelming relief wrapped around me
as I buried "us" a foot deeper than six from my heart
and two further from my mind.

I let us rest.

We were at peace.

But
when I started to move forward, cutting the last thread,
I found that you had resurrected
in thoughts and songs.

You would speak to me through dreams and faint echoes
that would softly play in my mind in the same way;
a broken record would repeat fifteen seconds of a single track.

You were gone, and you were with me.

You were dead to me and here…

…even in the ways that I move.

Anguish

Grief, to me, looked like 1 a.m.
in a dark room,
staring at the candle burning with two wicks.

One to represent me
and
the other to remind me of you.

I still don't know if watching it dwindle ever helped me,
or if it made reality sink in faster as I watched the wax soften
and the flames grow deeper into the jar.

But whatever it was,
it was felt so deeply that
it ran as smoothly as the blood through my veins.

It consumed me.

I became sorrow.

Just a Spider in Your Web

I was never really scared to leave.
The act of leaving in itself never instilled much fear;
it was the fact I knew you'd let me.

I knew you would let me get to that point of no return
where I walk out the door and take a deep breath.

I knew you would let me get halfway down
the path of getting over you
just to come back and knock on my door, wanting another chance.

You know my heart and all the ways in
which it is vulnerable to you.
You know that
my soft spot, my weakness, my muse is you.

I knew you would let me walk. That wasn't the hardest part.
I knew you would never let me truly leave.

The web you spun was too intricate for that.

Exploration and Discovery

The thing about my soul is that it loves to explore.

I welcome every opportunity
at a single moment closer to your aura
so I can relish in the moment.

I've grown comfortable
and maybe addicted
to traveling and navigating that territory.

I want to dive deeper. I need to search.

I want to find your mind,
taste your thoughts.
I crave undressing your mind in its entirety,
so I can promenade along the paths paved in memories.

Let me discover you.

Thunder for a Lullaby and Lightning for a Night-Light

He always liked when it stormed; he loved it…

…the darkness that it brought
along with the way
the wind would wisp
and whistle through the tree lines.

He liked the thunder and the crisp, cold air.

Maybe that's why he liked me,
even falling apart,
cracking in destruction, and bellowing out of anger,
he knew my love was rare.

That's Not Love

I grew tired of crying at least once a week
and claiming that was part of love.

I grew weak when you were away
but almost weaker the closer you became.

I grew fond of your heart, but I grew further
from pure intentions the deeper we dove.

You consumed me in ways that corrupted my morals.
You consumed me in ways that destroyed me.

Moonlight

What makes the night more cherished than the day?
Is it the glow of the moon?
Is it the way the trees sway?

The dancing shadows in the darkness, inviting sin,
the cold breeze that gently caresses your skin?

There's discretion in the way
the moon shines and shades.

I resemble her greatly
in many ways.

Weighed Down

The density of your soul pulls me,
and I am left with no choice but to gravitate toward you.

I require that gravity.
I invite that gravity
to push and pull me
in whichever way(s) necessary to bring me
closer
and closer

to you.

Wither

I loved you desperately.

In the pathetic way
of being dried out, abandoned, and
left parched.

Shriveling and shrinking from the lack of hydration,
I curled into myself more by the hour.

The desperation sets in for the smallest droplet of love
or anything that could be perceived as such
to help ease the drought.
Delusional to the point
I was unable to identify
the illusions I created were fictitious.
False.
Empty. Dry.
Barren.

You left me to my own devises.
You don't get to tell me I was wrong for
what I chose to do to survive.

Cruelty can lead people to dark places.

My Other Half

People are concerned for me,
telling me to be careful
and begging me not to get lost in you,

but with a wandering soul like mine,
you come to learn you're never lost.

You're simply wandering, discovering the hidden
wonders of the galaxies in your mind.

It took a matter of seconds for you to become my universe
in which everything revolved.

If only they knew I was never lost.

In fact, I discovered more of myself in you
than any other place I have ever been.

Please Remember Me

When the day comes that I have no tomorrow, do not forget me.

Do not forget the way I laughed in the rain and the
way the moonlight would dance in my eyes.
Do not forget the way my face felt, caressed
by your hand while I slept.
Do not forget the way I taste at two a.m., dancing
in the living room after three glasses of wine.
Do not forget the way I would sing in the
shower but only on the days I was sad.
Do not forget the way I was immersed
in awe of you simply existing.

But most importantly,

Do not ever forget the way I broke for you.
Willingly.
Happily.
Entirely.

Because I would do it over
a million times again.

You Didn't Even Slow Down

I guess what pissed me off most was that
I hesitated and you never did.

Every time I would walk out the door, I would hesitate.
I knew I couldn't leave you; I didn't want to.
I'd walk out just to turn around with the doorknob still in hand.

Every time I would get close to leaving,
I would catch myself in just enough time to stop.

I hesitated.

Every.
Single.
Time.

You never did. Not once.

Not when putting on your shoes,
tying the strings.
Not when walking toward the door while
letting words as sharp as knives
spiral from the part in your lips,
and certainly not when you opened the door and stormed out.

I knew I couldn't stop you.
I knew you were leaving,
but just once
I wish you would've slowed down.

You made it look so easy.

I hesitated every time.
Why did you never slow down?

My Feet Are Tired

Now you're left to follow the dust I leave behind.

It's your turn to try and catch up to me.

I'm done chasing.

The Second Door Can't Open
If the First Isn't Closed

Do not hesitate in closing the door.

Don't leave it cracked,
Unlocked,
or ajar.

Slam it shut
with purpose.

Choose you.

Well, Did You?

The moment I realized
I had reached insanity was
when I made you my happiness,
my light,
while you were taking that from me.

I gave so many chances,
hoping,
refusing to accept your actions
as my answer…

…thinking that if I just gave you one more,
you would change your mind.
You would stay.
You would choose me.

It eats at me,
wondering if you had ever planned to stay at all.

The Bandaged Wound

As soon as you left, I slapped on the Band-Aids.
Different sizes, shapes, and colors.

Whisky, sleep, notebooks filled with
all the things I had told you a million times but
still wished to tell you once more.

But see,
Band-Aids only adhere so long.
They only cover a "still healing" wound.

Patchwork is not reconstruction.

So the Band-Aids slip off after a few washes,
and I'm left staring
at the gashes that will scar in time,
remembering how that flesh looked before it was mutilated
at the hands of the one I loved most.

And as I stare, I wonder,
if I could see my heart,
just how many scars does she bear?

I've healed,
but these scars remind me.

You Are Not Silver

They promised you forever, and then left you in pieces,
didn't they?

That's okay.
Let them leave.

I know…
their last words are dancing in your head
like a never-ending ballet.
You're grasping at straws for
the slightest sign of hope
that maybe—somehow,
they'll come back.

I know
there's no one like them and you don't
know if you can ever love again,
but think about this with me:

What if they were holding you back from untapped potential
that you didn't even know you had?

Let them go so you can grow into the person
you've always dreamt of being.

Then after you've grown comfortable in that skin,
if they can handle you at your peak without
trying to take the credit,
without breaking you,
and you still want them while at your absolute strongest,
only then
can they come back.

So much can change in time. Focus on you, baby.

You are gold.
Don't let them mistake you for silver.

Don't Be Too Late

Can people change? Yes,

but here's the travesty:

more often than not, it is too late.

It's too late to love her the way she deserved.
It's too late to hold her one last time.
It's too late to try and right all your wrongs.
It's too late for "I'm sorry" and "Please just hold on."

The messiest things come from people who wait.
They say if it's worth it—if it's truly fate,
You won't mind the waiting or postponing the date,
but heartstrings grow tired;
elastic wears thin.

And now we're both stuck with the
"what could have been."

I Hope It Finds You

Sometimes we don't get what we want.

We don't find what we're looking for.

And sometimes,

what we *deserve*

finds us.

Hold Me Down, Do Not Confine Me

I knew who I was.

I never was the girl that craved perfection.
I didn't want the straight and narrow.

I didn't fancy the straight-laced and flawless.

I wanted someone respectful but firm,
someone unafraid to bark back and put me in my place.
At times, it was necessary
and still is.

I know who I am.

And though different from who I was, I
am easily two and a half handfuls
on a good day,
and I need someone to remind me

that while I do not have to stay inside the lines,
I do not always have to cross them.

I require your gravity.

In Perfect Harmony

I strode the lines of your heartstrings
as if they were a harp.

I plucked the right tune
as I gracefully grazed across you.

I treasured each step,
from gliding my hand with precision
before gently placing the other on your skin.

I not only had *you* convinced
but myself.

I absorbed your touch in the way the roots of trees absorb the water
that nurtures their growth and sustains their life.

We only made sense together.

Jet Lag

I grew weary of waiting

like a cigarette to be lit
or a book to be read,
a guitar on a stand
or a hand to be held.

I waited for the calls
and for the knocks on my door; neither of which came.

But one day, I woke up.

I was awakened and greeted with the question
that has been asked many times,

yet always refused to answer:

"What are you waiting for?"

The answer was always you,
but
the reality is scarce, if at all.

I grew weary of waiting,
of having my phone glued to my hand,
never wanting to miss a call, always worried
about the repercussions I may endure.
I was fatigued from the drama that surrounded you with lies and
all the sacrifices I made in order to keep us alive
when it was you cutting the stem, never allowing us to fully thrive.

I grew weary of waiting,

But I realized I was only waiting for my
strength to be shown through spirit.

Ink

You wear me on your body like your favorite jeans and
on your lips like your favorite brand of bourbon.

Both under each other and the influence of the other's charisma.

You put me on, and I become imprinted on your soul.

Compared to a disguised drug or creeping obliteration.

Almost fantasized.

Never divided. Never apart.
Maybe by life but never at heart.

For Me, It Will Always Be You

Yes, I became unsatisfied.
Unfulfilled.
Disappointed.

But even still,

I tried to keep us relevant.

For months, I worked tirelessly to prove to
myself that what we had was true.

It was, for me, this whole time, but
I'll always wonder if it really was for you.

I just wanted to feel like *we* still mattered.

Because for me, we always will.

Indebted

My heart had been sectioned
into poker chips,
and I would place my bet
each time
on hearts that were never mine.

Solely borrowed.
I found myself in undeniable debt at a young age…

…and we all know it's damn near impossible
to be debt-free in times like these.

Until We Meet Again

I closed my eyes during that kiss,
and even when I felt you loosen your grip on my face
and your hand slide down to my waist,
I still kept them closed.

In fact,
I clenched them that much more.

I knew what this was.
I could feel it in my heart.
This was goodbye.
This was the last time.

I knew you were going, but I couldn't bear to watch you leave.

I'm Still Yours

And if you ever wonder
if I have moved on,
if I have left you behind
and untangled my soul from yours,

I haven't.

I have always been remarkable at facades.

Don't forget.

Reverberation

It wasn't the scream that lingered
but the echo of our love.

It still plays on a loop to this day in my head,

and I still wonder

where it all went wrong.

Incomplete but Far from Imperfect

I will never be able to love myself
in the ways in which he loved me,
and that's why I will always feel like I need him.

He will always be missing from me,
with parts of me that I need
to be whole.

Are You Happy?

Sometimes I wonder if you knew from the beginning
that we were destined to stay connected
but damned to be apart.

I wonder if you knew as I did,
from that moment,
we would never be able to sever our souls.

I wonder if you knew you would have me
permanently, endlessly,
not even just physically
but my entirety—who I am.

All of me at your disposal at any time.

How does it feel?
I must know.

Living in the Future

As long as I have a pen and paper, you and I will never be done.
I refuse to write our ending.
We will never be finished.

The chapters may vary, and the stanzas may change,
but our book will never be finished.

You may be the chapter that I never read aloud,
but you are the one I still revisit
and reread.

It would be foolish to deny that ours was—
and still is—
my favorite.

I live in the words and bask in the joy and pray…
…for the future.

My Best Is Better with You

I know nothing truer than being
foolishly in love with you.

I am the most genuine version of myself
when you are loving me,

and

I am the truest when
I am loving you.

The Time Traveler's Point of View

I wish I could turn back time.

I don't wish to change anything,
only for us to have the opportunity to stand in the background
and watch ourselves fall in love with each other as each day goes by.

Our smiles.
Our laughs.
Our mornings in the kitchen and
our nights under sheets.

I wouldn't change any of it,
not even the arguments.

I simply wish to have the opportunity
to fall in love
with the way we fell in love with each other…again.

Compose Your Own Story

Everyone is a novel.
The genre will vary depending on where you are in life.

You do not solely fit into one category as
interests change.

Experience promotes growth.
Explorative by nature, it's only natural to broaden horizons.
So explore.
Extend.
Develop into what suits you…

…and do it unapologetically.

It's your book. Live every chapter without fear.

Tell Me

Do you remember who you were to me?

Am I still the same to you?

Just Curious

How far would you go for the thrill?

What avenues would you entertain?

Unarmed and Harmed

You may have pulled the trigger,

but I loaded that gun the minute I fell in love with you.

I surrendered it all to you.

All of my walls.

My mind, my weapon.

My secrets, your ammunition.

Thief

...of my mind,

then my heart,

then my sanity.

I'm Glad You're Okay

Conveniently for you,
we do not experience heartbreak in the same ways.

You recognize my absence,
but yours paralyzes me.

I Am Fleeting

I wanted to let you go, and I really needed to.
My friends and family kept telling me that
holding on to you was only killing me,
and I knew that.

What once were familiar eyes I would meet in a mirror
became empty,
unrecognizable—
as if my own reflection had become another stranger.

I met you when I was fragile.
Not yet broken but moments away.
You restored my faith and built me up; you made me stronger.

Though, I failed to see that strength only
existed when you were around.

Every time you went away, I could feel it—
like a lightning bolt so bright and vivid
yet brief and temporary.

Nothing will last if not with you, but I really need to let you go.

No Strings Attached (Anymore)

My thoughts—once like razor blades
cutting through my mind at excessive speeds—
have begun to slow.

Almost as if I cut myself lose from my own restrictions

finally.

Forcing Through

How obvious could it be?

I want to keep you in my story. I want your
name to monopolize each page,
but I have to move forward.

I have to. I don't have a choice.

I have to write the next chapter, and I have to leave you in this one.

Maybe there will be another in the future
in which your name dances once again
in black ink.

I pray that's true,

but for now,
I'll keep you here
and visit often.

It Will Always End with You

But even if I were to write a book
on my entire life,
the final sentence would still end with
you.

Fight(ing) for Me

I fought for the same things...

...over and over and over from you
while others were fighting
for me to give them one chance
to give me everything I
was wanting from you.

Let that sink in.

Met My Match

Salty rivers turn into oceans
as they stream down my cheeks
and embrace my chin.

Glowing embers burst into flames, and
I turn to ash

as I burn for you.

Building Blocks Aren't Stepping Stones

You were the most excruciating game of Jenga I had ever played.

We spent so much time building something so strong.
We took caution.
The effort in our precision,
placing each block as to ensure the reward would only be greater,
just to watch one piece sway
slowly but just strong enough to demolish
everything we had created.

I watched it fall
piece by piece
day by day.

and I thought,

What a waste.

Where Are You?

Who you love

and

who loves you

have a lot to do with what you are going through at the time.

Entrapment

You laughed at me and told me
you knew I'd never leave,
and through a silent crimson smile,
that's what I allowed you to believe.

Of all the tears I shed, I never let you see a drop.
I knew you only kept me there
as your favorite prop.

You were the puppeteer, but I still reign as the ringleader.
You were physically superior, but I was the best mind reader.

With a slight window of opportunity, I took my chance to flee.
You made my home a prison but forgot I had the key.

I'm finally free
(from you).

You Never Deserved Him

They say when it's your time
and you elect to let go,

you will no longer feel crippling pain
and
you will be free to grow.

From the moment I heard those words,
I knew
they were untrue.

I felt everything in multiples of twenties and thousands…
…watching him with you.

I Hope I Was Worth It

I was a chapter to you,
but you were the whole damn book to me.

The Past Can Creep up on You

I still believe we were made for each other.

Maybe not forever,
Maybe not to last,

but

you know as well as I do who we were…

…even if now we just label each other

"the past."

Nice to Meet You

I don't believe we've met, but
your lips are so familiar.
And my bed used to smell curiously similar
to the cologne on the collar of your polo.

I'm certain you don't remind me of anyone I've ever known, but
I have known those hands
and have found myself lost in your eyes well before now.

I am drawn to you,
and
I find myself wanting to confide in you.
But I think you already know
who I am.

I have journals full of stories
that have you written on every page—
from your clothes
to the way you walk
while simultaneously sipping bourbon on ice.

Maybe they weren't dreams.
Maybe you feel this too.

I don't believe we've met in this lifetime,
but I'm certain we've met before—

maybe in another life. But allow me to
reintroduce myself in this one.

I'm glad I found you.
I almost feel compelled to tell you I've missed you.

Let's fall in love again.

Better the First Time Around

I am not one to be saved for later;
I've found I go stale.

I Never Meant to Be So Reckless with You

I think you always knew
when you looked into my eyes
that you truly made me happy, but
you just weren't the "right" guy.

I could tell you were desperate
to be the one I called my life,
but the truth is that you always knew
I was only halfway your wife.

I knew you could feel it
in the way I moved my lips;
I was kissing you with my eyes closed
while thinking about his.

I apologize,
for you were a casualty
to my forever shattered heart.
You got sliced on edges of glass
that eventually slit us apart.

Time Heals?

"Do you feel relieved at all?" my friend asked—
and asked in a hopeful tone.

She wanted me to feel some peace and hope so I could move on.

Feeling a little pressure, I forcefully pushed out the words,

"A little.

I miss him, though, and when I do,

I still feel my heart get brittle."

I present a strong exterior because that's what people want,

but truthfully, I feel breathless.

I'll always miss him.

He was my "one."

Losing Game

I was the girl that needed constant reassurance,
and
you were the boy that never knew how to
express feelings through words.

It was our fate to lose the war before we started the battle,

but we sure gave it hell.

Year of Seasons

Your smile is spring,
and your tears,
winter.

Let me explain how you beam summer rays when you're laughing.

Always growing and changing like the leaves of fall.

You were but one season in my life yet gave me all.

I am so thankful for you.

She Sleeps

It got to the point where she couldn't even sleep to escape.

Crowded dreams made what was supposed to be peaceful
so very taxing.

She was stuck reliving the same day in her mind.
The same thoughts, the same battles and demons—
every day, the same mountains to climb.

Seemingly, there was no relief to be found.

She cried.
She ached.
She begged and screamed.

Then she realized,

it was not sleep that she was deprived of
but peace.

A soul deprived of rest results in
a mind deprived of ease.

And after realizing that,
she now finally sleeps.

I Miss Being the Passenger in Your Car

Streetlights don't look the same from my driver's seat
as they do in the passenger seat of your car,
nor do the stars
nor the moon.

And my smile is not as wide;
my eyes are not as focused as they once were when resting on yours.

I miss that feeling, and I feel empty.
How can a sight make you *feel?*

I miss the way we were together,
and I hate the way nothing else seems real.

They Never Made Sense

He was thunderstorms, and she hated rain.

He hated oceans, and she was a hurricane.

I Never Doubted the Love

I always knew you loved me too…

…it was just never in the same way that I loved you

was it, love?

Irrational Optimism

Hoping for you felt
like hoping for a rose bush to spontaneously bloom in abundance
in a desert.

It was disappointing,
foolish,
and filled me with despair.

I never needed you more than in the moments you never showed.

From Your Perspective: I Still See Through Your Lens

Planted in pain,

I watched my other half become whole again with another.

I saw that look in her eyes once again, but
I was no longer in the reflection.

As much as it pained me, though,

she smiled,
so I smiled too.

I knew she'd have so much to tell me
when we reunited to start new.

How Long Is Forever?

I guess when he said he would love me "forever," it was relative.

He only meant *his* forever, not mine.

It was always on his time,

not mine.

Reminisce

Don't forget the mornings before the sun was awake,
baking cookies in only a T-shirt,

and

don't forget the afternoons we spent
day-drunk in a dugout off a gravel road, staring at the clouds,

and

don't forget the nights before the moon tucked us in,
dancing and being found in the other's eyes.

My favorite parts of the days are the ones I spent with you.

Value(d) Myself

Trapped in disbelief,
I walked in and found myself in shambles on the bathroom floor,
mostly still drunk from the night before.

I thought I was reliving a memory, but that was not what this was.

It must have been an out-of-body experience, I thought.
Confused, I wondered, "How am I here?"

I could hear myself saying,
"You're only hurting yourself,
you can't drown your thoughts and longing."

"But I'm desperate and aching."

Yet I still hear myself saying,
"Get up. You can't stay here. *Feel* so you can *heal.*"

It was then that I realized,
I needed no knight, no prince, no white horse…
The only thing I needed was to remind *myself*

that I was worth so much more.

Only for You

Endlessly enough is all I ever craved to be.

Now Embers Once Ablaze

For years, I left a match under my doormat
in hope that you'd come back and want
to strike up our old flame.

You lit the match, and my eyes glistened in its essence,

only to realize

you came to burn my house down…

…and that the empty hope
is why I was always your fool.

One More Won't Hurt

The thought of
Just one more
almost killed me in reference to you.

One more text.
One more call.
One more touch.
One more kiss.
One more night.
One more meal.
One more laugh.
One more memory.
One more moment.

I caved every time at the mere thought of
one more of anything with you.

I only let go after realizing there will never only be one more,
and I cannot add them all up to fill the void of my lifetime.

You are everything and nothing to me.

I am nothing and everything to you.

Steeplechase

"You'll be the death of me, girl," you said
as you slowly lifted your gaze to meet mine.

I'd crack a smile, and you'd shoot me a wink.

We were off to the races after that.

I lost track of who was ahead;
I still don't know who won,

but man,

we certainly enjoyed the ride.

Hope

I don't know who I'll be ten years from now,

but I hope you love her too.

About the Author

Hannah G. Milan, author of *The Healing*

Hannah G. Milan was born and raised outside the city of Columbus, in the beautiful "Crossroads of America" state, Indiana. Growing up, Hannah has always found a way to be a helping hand to others. She found that she could help others while being creative and expressive through her writing. Hannah usually writes early in the morning or much later in the evenings. Hannah considers her faith and family to be most important to her. If she isn't spending time with her friends and family, you can almost always find her around her sweet black-and-white American shorthair tuxedo cat, Max. *The Healing* is Hannah's first published book.

CPSIA information can be obtained
at www.ICGtesting.com
Printed in the USA
LVHW030807211122
733624LV00009B/701